the Kings and Queens
of
England and Great Britain
Colouring Book

Copyright © 2021 Joseph Stephen

ISBN-13: 978-84-122325-7-8

COVER IMAGE: Based on St Edward's Crown, Royal Collection Trust

For more information on
MadeGlobal Publishing, visit our website
www.madeglobal.com

M

MadeGlobal Publishing

ACKNOWLEDGEMENTS

I want to thank Tim at MadeGlobal for this incredible opportunity
and my wonderful girlfriend Lumi for all the support.
It has been a dream for me to work on and publish this book,
and I hope you get as much enjoyment out of
reading and colouring it as I did in creating it.

Joseph Stephen

This book belongs to

○○

Table of Contents

THE STUARTS

THE HOUSE OF HANOVER

THE HOUSE OF WINDSOR

THE
NORMANS
1066-1154

KING WILLIAM I (WILLIAM THE CONQUEROR)

REIGNED: 1066-1087

WILLIAM was one of the most formidable warriors in Europe and a distant cousin of King Edward the Confessor. Born the illegitimate son of the Duke of Normandy and a tanner's daughter, William earned the nickname 'William the Bastard'. Despite his illegitimacy, he became the Duke of Normandy after his father's death in 1035. William gained a reputation for both ruthlessness and bravery and conquered much of northern France as duke.

William claimed that Edward the Confessor had promised him the English throne in 1051. In 1066, Harold Godwinson was crowned King of England. That same year, the Pope showed support for William's claim to the English throne.

On 28th September 1066, William, Duke of Normandy, landed on the southeast coast of England, ready to fight for the English crown. His Norman army numbered ten thousand men, with three thousand knights on horseback. The Norman army marched ten miles inland to Hastings, and Harold Godwinson's Saxon army marched two hundred miles from Stamford Bridge to the south coast.

At 9 a.m. on 14th October 1066, the two armies met outside Hastings. William's army struggled to break through the Saxon shield wall. After hours of fighting, William called retreat. Harold was overjoyed, and his army broke out of formation to chase and kill the retreating Norman soldiers. However, the Norman retreat had been a trick. William ordered it to tempt the Saxon soldiers away from the high ground and break their shield wall. The Normans now regrouped and picked off the disorganised Saxon army. King Harold was killed on the battlefield. William, Duke of Normandy, was now 'William the Conqueror'.

On Christmas Day 1066, two months after he had defeated Harold, William was crowned King William I of England at Westminster Abbey.

KING WILLIAM II

REIGNED: 1087-1100

WILLIAM WAS THE SECOND SON of William the Conqueror. His father did not get on with any of his sons. The empire that stretched across Normandy and England, by right, should have passed onto his eldest brother, Robert. However, his father disliked Robert. Before his death, William the Conqueror gave England to his middle son, William; Normandy to his eldest son, Robert, and 5000 pounds to his youngest son, Henry.

William II was angry, short-tempered, and often offended the Church through his open disdain for religion. He was nicknamed 'Rufus' by his subjects for his red hair.

In August 1100, William II was out hunting with his close friend, Walter Tirel. Tirel was known for being a good archer, but when shooting at a stag, Tirel missed and hit King William II straight in the chest. The king dropped to the floor and is said to have died instantly from the arrow wound. Tirel fled to France, where he died in exile later that year. Historians and scholars have often wondered whether the death of King William II was an accident or deliberately planned.

KING HENRY I

REIGNED: 1100-1135

WILLIAM II'S YOUNGER BROTHER, HENRY, was at the same hunt as the king and Tirel. On hearing of his brother's death, Henry acted quickly and rode to Winchester. Three days later, Henry was crowned King Henry I.

Six years later, Henry I captured his eldest brother, Robert, the Duke of Normandy, on the battlefield in Normandy. Henry seized Robert's French lands and imprisoned him in Cardiff Castle for thirty years, until his death. Through imprisoning his oldest brother and potentially killing his other brother, Henry had gone from inheriting 5000 pounds and ruling nothing, to ruling over the whole of his father's empire.

With his two brothers out of the way, King Henry I married Princess Matilda. Together, they had one son named William, but he died in 1120.

Henry I ruled England for thirty-five peaceful years until his death in 1135. Henry died without issue.

KING STEPHEN

REIGNED: 1135-1154

HENRY I'S DEATH threw England into disarray and conflict. In the absence of a direct male heir, two cousins lay claim to the English throne: Henry's daughter, Empress Matilda, and his nephew, Stephen.

Stephen was a friendly, well-liked figure among the Anglo-Norman nobility, whereas Matilda was disliked and seen as arrogant. Moreover, few Norman lords were prepared to be ruled by a woman. Thus, although Matilda was Henry I's child, Stephen was crowned King Stephen of England in December 1135.

Stephen and Matilda's rival claims to the throne of England threw the country into a nineteen-year civil war. Law and order completely broke down. The nation was in chaos. Great areas of the country had no royal authority, leaving the people at the mercy of cruel, sometimes tyrannical, barons. For this reason, King Stephen's reign and this period is remembered as 'The Anarchy'.

THE PLANTAGENETS
1154-1399

KING HENRY II

REIGNED: 1154-1189

HENRY II's mother was Empress Matilda. Towards the end of 'The Anarchy', Matilda agreed to allow her cousin Stephen to rule, provided her son, Henry, would succeed Stephen as king. Stephen agreed. In 1154, King Stephen died. Henry was crowned King Henry II. After nineteen years of civil war, Henry II was determined to restore peace and order to England.

Henry II was the first Plantagenet monarch in England. He was a great fighter on the battlefield and won back land that had been lost to Wales and Scotland during the reign of King Stephen. As well as ruling England and Normandy, he gained Anjou through his father, the Count of Anjou, and Aquitaine through his marriage to Eleanor of Aquitaine. Henry's territory was known as the 'Angevin Empire'. It stretched from the border with Scotland in the north to the Pyrenees in southern France.

Henry II's reign, which started so well, ended in sadness. Three of Henry's eldest sons were angry that he would not share control of the Angevin Empire. Along with their mother, Queen Eleanor, his sons led an uprising against his rule. Their revolt failed. As punishment, Henry II threw his wife, Eleanor, into prison. Henry never properly made peace with any of his sons, and they continued to rebel against his rule.

In 1189, Henry travelled to the place of his youth, Chinon, where he was told of the fall of Tours to his eldest son, Richard. On hearing that his favourite son, John, had joined Richard in revolt against him, Henry cried, 'I no longer care for anything in this world'. Henry II died in 1189. Before his death, he named his eldest surviving son, Richard, as his successor.

KING RICHARD I

REIGNED: 1189-1199

RICHARD WAS CROWNED KING RICHARD I at Westminster in September 1189. Once crowned, he welcomed his mother, Eleanor of Aquitaine, back to court. Within a year of his coronation, Richard left England for Palestine on a crusade to the Holy Land. With his older brother away, John tried to steal Richard's crown and become King of England.

On returning to England from Palestine, Richard was captured and imprisoned by the Duke of Austria. John was asked to pay Richard's ransom but refused. Determined to take the crown for himself, John even told the English people that Richard had been killed abroad on crusade.

In 1194, Richard returned to England. In a show of mercy, he forgave John for betraying him and did not sentence him to death.

Richard only remained in England for a brief time. He travelled to France and spent the remaining five years of his life fighting the French. Richard died on the battlefield in France from blood poisoning when a crossbow wound went septic. Magnanimously, Richard pardoned his killer on his deathbed.

Richard I was known as 'Richard the Lionheart' for his bravery on the battlefield. He had one illegitimate son, Philip of Cognac, but died with no legitimate heir.

KING JOHN

REIGNED: 1199-1216

JOHN ASCENDED TO THE THRONE upon his older brother Richard's death. John was a short man, standing at 5'5". He was nicknamed Lackland for holding no lands or territory. It was argued strongly for Richard's twelve-year-old nephew, Arthur, to succeed to the throne instead of John. The barons disagreed with this. They had no affection for John, but understood the importance of heredity and the line of succession. They also did not want another civil war to engulf the country.

John had disagreements with the Pope about who should be the next Archbishop of Canterbury. Due to this, the Pope excommunicated John in 1209 and ordered an 'interdict', meaning that no English church could marry couples, hold services, baptise children or bury dead bodies. The 'interdict' lasted for five years. The populace was furious and feared they would go straight to hell.

John suffered several military defeats. He lost Anjou, Brittany, and, most embarrassingly, the family's ancestral home of Normandy. By 1204, he had lost one-third of the Angevin Empire. Finally, in 1214, John assembled an army to win back land lost in France, but experienced a crushing defeat at the Battle of Bouvines.

The English Barons were not happy. They had paid enormous taxes for John to raise an army, but he kept losing. Finally, in 1215, the barons marched to London to meet King John and confronted him with a list of demands. These demands included not trying to control the English church, not raising tax without the barons' permission and not imprisoning people without a fair trial. John signed the list of demands by royal seal, and it became known as the 'Magna Carta'.

Shortly after signing the Magna Carta, John declared the document invalid. The barons were furious. They marched to London and declared that John should no longer rule as king. By autumn 1215, England was engulfed in civil war. One year later, in October 1216, King John went to bed suffering from an upset stomach and died during the night.

KING HENRY III

REIGNED: 1216-1272

HENRY III ascended to the throne upon the death of his father, John, when he was only nine years old. For the first decade of young Henry's reign, state affairs passed to Hubert de Burgh, who was like a father figure to the young monarch.

Like his uncle, Richard I, Henry craved glory in battle. But, unlike his uncle, he was not a good soldier. Henry set sail to retrieve his grandfather's (Henry II) French possessions lost by King John. It was a venture in which he failed, and at a great human cost.

Henry gave London its first zoo, kept at the Tower of London.

In 1252, Henry made a tactical error and dismissed his brother-in-law, Simon de Montfort. De Montfort was frustrated by his dismissal. He publicly voiced his frustration and began to oppose the king. He quickly attracted support from the barons, the City of London and the clergy, who were all distressed by Henry's 'alien monarchy'. De Montfort created a council of fifteen who met three times a year, whether or not summoned by the monarch. Under de Montfort, England had had its first taste of parliamentary rule.

Henry III died in 1272, having ruled for fifty-six years. His reign was to prove a high point in the medieval power of Parliament and barons.

KING EDWARD I

REIGNED: 1272-1307

Edward I'S FATHER, Henry III, spent much of his reign fighting with his barons. For this reason, Edward I spent much of his youth on the battlefield at war.

The English people welcomed Edward after the unhappy reigns of his father, Henry III, and grandfather, John. He was charismatic, good looking and had a loving marriage to his queen, Eleanor of Castille. He was extremely tall for his time. Standing at 6'2", King Edward was known as 'Longshanks' by his soldiers, meaning 'Long Legs'.

Edward and Eleanor had sixteen children together.

Edward led successful military campaigns in Wales and Scotland. In just twenty-one days, he defeated the Scots, earning him the nickname the 'Hammer of Scots'.

Edward developed dysentery in 1307. On 6th July that year, he died in his servants' arms when they came to lift him to feed him.

KING EDWARD II

EDWARD II was so unlike his warrior father, Edward I, that some questioned his paternity. He ascended to the throne aged twenty-three and, at the time of his accession, was in the process of marrying Isabella, the twelve-year-old daughter of the King of France.

Soon after their marriage, Isabella was concerned by Edward's very close relationship with his friend, Piers Gaveston. To protect the crown and monarch from any public indignity, the king's council banished and killed Gaveston. Edward was grief-stricken. The king kept Gaveston's corpse at his side for weeks, until it was dragged away.

Gaveston was replaced in the king's affections by the unpopular Hugh Despenser. Despenser was granted the earldom of Gloucester. The barons of England were furious that such a large area of land had been granted to Despenser, and as a result, the baronial wars against the king resumed.

The barons acquired the support of Edward's now estranged wife, Isabella. Together, they forced Edward II and Despenser to flee to the West Country. Both were captured, and Despenser was executed. However, Isabella and the barons faced a problem with Edward: how to dispose of a legitimate king anointed in the name of God. They could not just execute the reigning monarch.

The barons and Isabella sought the advice of the bishops, who advised that the head of state could not be deposed, but only invited to abdicate. Edward II was propositioned to abdicate and tearfully agreed to this, provided his fourteen-year-old son by Isabella, also named Edward, would succeed him. Edward's son was crowned King of England, and Edward II was moved to Berkeley Castle, where he was murdered later that year.

KING EDWARD III

REIGNED: 1327-1377

EDWARD III was not like his father. He was a brilliant soldier and is considered one of the great generals in English history. He enjoyed acting, and in his early days as monarch would dress up as Sir Lancelot. He was routinely at war with Ireland and Scotland, but these wars paled in comparison to those with France.

In 1328, King Charles IV of France died without issue. Edward III's mother and King Charles's sister, Isabella, claimed the French throne for her son. Philip of Valois, Charles's cousin, also claimed the French throne. After several disputes, Philip ascended to the French throne as king.

In 1337, Edward and Philip declared themselves at war over the French throne. In 1340, Edward's forces defeated Philip VI's French forces for control of the Channel. This began what was called the Hundred Years' War. Edward's first major invasion of France in 1346 took over ten thousand English troops to the gates of Paris. Still, its walls proved impenetrable to arrows, and the English were decimated by dysentery.

In 1356, the then King of France, John II, was captured at the Battle of Poitiers and brought to the Tower of London. Edward was winning the battle for the French throne, but at the same time, disease was rife among Edward's troops in France. As a result, thousands of soldiers were dying from dysentery and other diseases. This forced Edward III to sign the Treaty of Brétigny in 1360. This treaty enabled England to recover a large portion of land in northwestern France once owned by King Henry II.

Edward III founded the Order of the Garter in 1348. In the same year, the Black Death reduced the population of England from five and a half million to four million.

Edward III's son and heir apparent, Edward the Black Prince, predeceased his father. This meant that when Edward III died in 1377, the Black Prince's son, and Edward's grandson, Richard, ascended to the throne.

KING RICHARD II

REIGNED: 1377-1399

RICHARD II is often compared to his great-grandfather, Edward II. Neither was well suited to medieval monarchy and both had male favourites.

In 1382, Richard married Anne of Bohemia, but the king seemed to pay more attention to one of his male courtiers, Robert de Vere, Marquis of Oxford.

In 1397, Richard exiled the Duke of Gloucester, Henry Bolingbroke. This left the previously loyal Bolingbroke enraged. To make matters worse, Richard II confiscated the entire Lancastrian estate that was promised to Bolingbroke.

In 1399, Richard left England for Ireland with a small army to end a rebellion. This allowed Bolingbroke to return to England from exile. Bolingbroke quickly amassed an army and intercepted Richard in North Wales. Bolingbroke took the king prisoner, and Richard II was forced to abdicate or face death. Bolingbroke was crowned King Henry IV.

Richard was imprisoned in Pontefract Castle, and in February 1400 was found dead, probably through starvation.

THE HOUSE OF LANCASTER 1399-1471

KING HENRY IV

REIGNED: 1399-1413

HENRY IV was the first monarch of the House of Lancaster. Henry might have been a crowned and anointed king, but he was an unpopular monarch. He was viewed by many as a usurper with his imprisoned predecessor, Richard II, still alive in Pontefract Castle at the beginning of his reign. Such a situation tore at the stability of the country.

Because of how he acquired power, Henry IV spent much of his reign fighting and quelling revolts. In 1400, Welsh landowner Owain Glyndŵr called on the Welsh to rebel against the monarch. The Welsh revolt dragged on until 1409, when the rebels were defeated, and the rebel fortress of Harlech fell to Henry's son, the future King Henry V.

Henry IV was consumed by ill health at the end of his life. Due to the adversity and backlash he had sustained throughout his reign, Henry was obsessed with plots against his throne and extremely paranoid. Finally, in March 1413, Henry collapsed in Westminster Abbey after suffering from a terrible skin condition, thought to be leprosy. He died in the Jerusalem Chamber of Westminster Abbey, fulfilling a prophecy that he would die 'in Jerusalem'.

KING HENRY V

REIGNED: 1413-1422

UPON HIS FATHER HENRY IV'S DEATH IN 1413, Henry V was crowned King of England. Henry knew that he had to work hard to win the support of the English people after the tumultuous reign of his father. Therefore, Henry V restored titles, lands, and castles to nobles who had opposed his father.

Henry V was the first King of England to conduct his court in English, not French. The Hundred Years' War, started during the reign of Edward III, continued during Henry V's reign. England had lost all of its lands in France except for Calais. However, France was ruled by a mad king, King Charles VI. With a mad monarch in charge, Henry V saw this as the perfect opportunity to invade France. Henry crossed the Channel with twelve thousand men and successfully took the French port of Harfleur.

On the road to Calais from Harfleur, Henry V won the Battle of Agincourt. This battle is still remembered today as one of the greatest victories in English military history. At this battle, eight thousand Englishmen defeated twelve thousand Frenchmen. The French were slaughtered. Around five thousand Frenchmen are thought to have died, compared to only about one thousand six hundred Englishmen.

Henry V won a series of battles in France after the Battle of Agincourt. By 1420, Henry was closing in on Paris. At this point, he could have won the French throne by force but instead signed the Treaty of Troyes with Charles VI. The treaty agreed that Henry V would marry Charles VI's daughter, Catherine of Valois, and on Charles's death, Henry V would become King of France. Unfortunately, Henry V died of dysentery in 1422, one month before Charles VI died.

KING HENRY VI

REIGNED: 1422-1461 AND 1470-1471

HENRY VI, son of King Henry V and Catherine of Valois, was England's youngest ever king. He was just nine months old at his accession in 1422. A royal council governed England on his behalf for the first sixteen years of his life.

When Henry VI came of age, he fell well short of the great expectations set by his military hero father, Henry V. England had been steadily losing its French territories to a new powerful French monarch, King Charles VII. Like his father, Henry V, Henry VI was expected to lead the English army into war against the French. This never happened. Instead, Henry VI sent his cousin to lead his armies against the French. Henry VI hated the idea of war and was the first medieval monarch never to lead his army on the battlefield. Because of this, many of Henry's noblemen and subjects believed he was a coward.

By 1450, England's French empire was once again reduced to Calais. This caused outrage and riots on the streets of London.

Henry suffered from bouts of madness in the 1450s. As a result, it was clear that he was not fit to rule as monarch. A group of powerful nobles, one of whom was the king's cousin, Richard, Duke of York, decided to take control of the nation's affairs. Henry's wife, Margaret of Anjou, despised Richard, and she began to organise opposition to the Duke of York. This opposition led to a division in the king's court. The supporters of the Duke of York were on one side, and the supporters of the king, led by his wife, Queen Margaret, were on the other side.

In 1459, Margaret declared Richard, Duke of York, a traitor. As a result, war broke out between the House of York and the House of Lancaster. Today, this war is famously known as the Wars of the Roses; the red rose of Lancaster versus the white rose of York.

Queen Margaret defeated the Duke of York at the Battle of Wakefield in December 1460. Richard was cornered and beheaded on the battlefield by Lancastrian troops. Richard's head was placed on a spike outside the gates of York and adorned with a paper crown as a warning to any would-be usurpers.

The House of York
York
1461-1485

KING EDWARD IV

REIGNED: 1461-1470 AND 1471-1483

QUEEN MARGARET'S victory and success were short-lived. The people of London refused to allow her into the city, so she fled to the North of England. Meanwhile, Edward, son of Richard, Duke of York, took on the leadership of the House of York.

Edward was everything that mad King Henry VI was not. He was young, charismatic, a proven warrior on the battlefield and very tall, standing at 6'4".

In March 1461, Edward was crowned King Edward IV of England. He marched north and finished off the Lancastrian forces. Henry VI and Queen Margaret fled to Scotland in exile. Edward IV secured his place as the first Yorkist King of England.

In 1464, Edward married his true love in secret, a commoner named Elizabeth Woodville. Such a marriage was unheard of for a king. Kings were expected to marry into another royal family to form a tactical alliance. On hearing this news, the Earl of Warwick, who had groomed Edward to be king from an early age and was the true power behind the throne, switched sides from the House of York to the House of Lancaster. In 1470, Warwick invaded England with Queen Margaret and won.

King Edward IV fled to Flanders, and Warwick reinstated Henry VI as King of England once more. Thus, a monarch from the House of Lancaster once again ruled over the nation.

King Henry VI's second reign was short-lived and only lasted one year. In 1471, at the Battle of Barnet, Edward IV's Yorkist army defeated Henry's Lancastrian army, and the Earl of Warwick was killed. Henry VI was captured and imprisoned. Henry later died in prison, most likely murdered by Edward's soldiers. King Henry VI was the last king of the House of Lancaster.

King Edward IV ruled England in relative peace for twelve more years. Then, in 1483, Edward was out fishing and caught a cold. He died a few days later at just forty years old.

KING EDWARD V

REIGNED: 1483

EDWARD IV AND ELIZABETH WOODVILLE had two young sons at the time of Edward's death. The eldest son and heir apparent, also named Edward, was due to become King Edward V. As he was only twelve years old, Edward's uncle, Richard, Duke of Gloucester, who was Edward IV's younger brother, was chosen to rule as lord protector on the young king's behalf.

In 1483, Richard imprisoned the two young princes in the Tower of London when they arrived back in the capital from Ludlow. Richard claimed it was for the princes' protection, but it soon turned out that Richard himself was the greatest threat to the princes' safety.

Edward V was never crowned king. As lord protector, Richard declared the marriage between his older brother, King Edward IV, and Elizabeth Woodville invalid. Prince Edward and his younger brother were now illegitimate. As Edward IV's younger brother, Richard was now next in the line of succession for the English throne. Richard then had himself crowned king as King Richard III.

Once placed in the Tower, the two sons of Edward IV were never seen again. To this day, it is believed that Richard III murdered his two nephews. Over two hundred years later, in 1674, workers in the Tower of London found a wooden chest hidden beneath a staircase containing two skeletons. The skeletons were of two children, one slightly older than the other. It was concluded at the time that the skeletons belonged to the two princes, and they were re-interred in Westminster Abbey.

KING RICHARD III

REIGNED: 1483-1485

EVEN IN 1483, rumours began to spread that Richard III had murdered his two nephews. This was thought of as an unthinkable act, even in the brutal context of the Wars of the Roses.

Richard III ruled England for two years. Then, in 1485, an unlikely new claimant to the English throne emerged, Henry Tudor. Henry's Welsh grandfather was a servant to King Henry V named Owain ap Maredudd ap Tewdwr. In 1432, Owain married the widow of Henry V, Catherine of Valois, and anglicised his name to Owen Tudor. They had a son, Edmund Tudor (Henry Tudor's father), the half-brother of King Henry VI.

Henry Tudor was a member of the House of Lancaster. He had spent fourteen years in exile in France, preparing his bid for the English throne. Henry was helped greatly by his formidable mother, Margaret Beaufort, who was the great-great-granddaughter of King Edward III.

In August 1485, Richard III and Henry Tudor met at the Battle of Bosworth Field. Outnumbered and poorly positioned at the foot of the hill in a marshy bog, there was little reason to expect Henry's Lancastrian forces to win. Richard III led the Yorkist cavalry charge against the Lancastrian forces, but one of Henry's men knocked Richard off his horse. Richard III was cornered, overpowered and killed.

Richard's gold crown was found in a thorn bush and placed on Henry Tudor's head. Meanwhile, Richard's corpse was stripped naked and slung on the back of a horse. In September 2012, archaeologists found what is believed to be Richard III's skeleton beneath a car park in Leicester. In March 2015, Richard III was given a king's funeral and burial at Leicester Cathedral.

Richard III was the last monarch of the House of York. His defeat and death at the Battle of Bosworth Field marked the end of the Middle Ages in England.

This colouring page is based on the famous portrait of Richard by an unknown artist.

THE
TUDORS
1485-1603

KING HENRY VII

REIGNED: 1485-1509

HENRY VII was crowned King of England in 1485. The Wars of the Roses were over. In a final act of unity between the House of York and the House of Lancaster, Henry VII married Elizabeth of York, daughter of King Edward IV and elder sister to the Princes in the Tower. The well-judged marriage united the red rose of Lancaster with the white rose of York, creating the red and white Tudor Rose. The Tudor Rose still adorns churches, castles, buildings and palaces across England to this day. The Tudor Rose can be seen in the background of the picture of Henry VII on the opposite page of this book.

Henry VII was an intelligent and calculating king. He enjoyed administration and personally signed thousands of documents which are still stored in the National Archives today. Additionally, he was very financially aware. He implemented several different strategies during his reign to generate revenue and coin.

During Henry VII's reign, there were revolts and rebellions. Henry was challenged by pretenders Perkin Warbeck and Lambert Simnel, who claimed to be Richard, Duke of York, one of the Princes in the Tower, and Edward Plantagenet, son of the Duke of Clarence. On both occasions, Henry VII saw off his enemies and secured a lasting peace for England.

In 1501, Henry VII yielded a great diplomatic triumph by marrying his oldest son Arthur to Catherine of Aragon. This marriage secured a powerful Anglo-Spanish tactical alliance. Although this was the case, Arthur died suddenly at Ludlow Castle within six months of the marriage. In 1509, Henry VII died. He was buried in a casket of splendour at Westminster Abbey. Henry had learned that majesty required splendour, even in death.

This colouring page is based on the very well known portrait of Henry by an unknown Netherlandish artist.

KING HENRY VIII

REIGNED: 1509-1547

FOLLOWING THE DEATH OF HIS FATHER, Henry VII, Henry, Duke of York, was crowned King Henry VIII in 1509 in a joint coronation with his new bride, his brother's widow, Catherine of Aragon. At first, the couple was very happy, but this did not last. Catherine became pregnant six times, but only one child survived infancy, a daughter called Mary. In 1519, Henry's mistress, Bessie Blount, gave birth to a healthy son, Henry Fitzroy. By 1525, Catherine was too old to have any more children, and Henry knew this.

Henry VIII craved to have a son and heir. The king became infatuated with one of his wife's maids of honour, Anne Boleyn. Henry tried to flirt with Anne, but she ignored him. Henry even offered Anne the title of his official mistress, but she declined. He then offered her marriage and she accepted. Henry told Catherine that he wanted to annul their marriage, but Catherine did not agree.

Henry asked Pope Clement VII for an annulment, but the pope refused to grant the king an annulment. After years of struggling to obtain an annulment, Henry decided to break with Rome's authority and make himself head of the Church in England. He passed the Act of Supremacy, making him the Supreme Head of the Church in England. The break from the authority of the pope and Rome by the Church of England was the beginning of the English Reformation. In 1533, Henry VIII married Anne Boleyn, and his marriage to Catherine was declared invalid.

In 1533, Anne had her first child, a girl called Elizabeth, and then, in 1534, had a miscarriage or stillbirth. In early 1536, Henry began to spend more time with one of Anne's ladies in waiting, Jane Seymour, and not long after, Anne had a miscarriage. She had failed to give Henry the son he so desperately wanted. Henry informed Cromwell that he wanted to get rid of Anne. Anne Boleyn was sent to the Tower of London, accused of taking other men as lovers, including her brother, and plotting to kill the king. Anne was found guilty and executed. The next day, Henry announced his engagement to Jane Seymour.

Jane Seymour gave Henry the son he had always wanted, Prince Edward. Henry rejoiced; however, his joy would quickly turn to sadness, as twelve days later, Jane Seymour died.

Henry VIII fathered no more children. He married three more times: to Anne of Cleves, to Catherine Howard and to Catherine Parr. Henry VIII died in 1547, aged fifty-five. He was buried next to his 'favourite' wife, Jane Seymour, in a vault at St George's Chapel at Windsor Castle.

This colouring page is based on the famous Hans Holbein portrait of Henry VIII from 1536-1537.

KING EDWARD VI

REIGNED: 1547-1553

EDWARD was only nine when his father, Henry VIII, died, and he inherited the throne.

Even though Henry VIII was the Supreme Head of the Church of England, he had still thought of himself as Catholic. Additionally, the majority of England still thought of themselves as Catholic during Henry's reign, regardless of the Reformation. However, Henry allowed his son, Edward VI, to be brought up by Protestants. Edward believed deeply in the Protestant faith. He believed the Catholic Church made people worship in the wrong way. Edward believed that God should be worshipped in a plain and simple manner, and, as head of the Church, he had the power to change this. Edward was too young to rule on his own, so the country was governed first by Edward Seymour, Duke of Somerset, and then John Dudley, Duke of Northumberland. These two men were Reformers and started to make England a truly Protestant country.

Many people did not like all the changes to the way they worshipped. They loved the old services and churches, and in some areas, there were rebellions.

In 1552, Edward's health was severely affected by smallpox and measles, and in 1553, at the age of fifteen, Edward lay dying of tuberculosis.

Edward knew he was dying, and the childless king wrote instructions naming his first cousin once removed, Lady Jane Grey, as his heir, and removing his half-sisters, Mary and Elizabeth, from the line of succession. This was done to prevent the country's return to Catholicism.

King Edward VI died on 6th July 1553.

This colouring page is based on the famous William Scrots portrait of Edward VI from around 1546-1547.

LADY JANE GREY

REIGNED: 6TH - 19TH JULY 1553

FOUR DAYS AFTER HIS DEATH, Edward's command was enacted, and Lady Jane Grey became the de facto queen.

Lady Jane was a devout Protestant. Edward's older half-sister, Mary, who was devoutly Catholic, fled to Framlingham Castle on hearing that her half-brother was dying. There, an uprising supporting Mary's claim to the throne won wide support.

Roughly ten thousand armed men advanced on London in support of Mary and her claim to the throne of England. The Duke of Northumberland and Lady Jane Grey had just a small force at their disposal to battle Mary's army. Realising that he could not defeat Mary's forces, the Duke of Northumberland soon capitulated and accepted Mary as Queen of England. Northumberland was beheaded, and Lady Jane Grey was imprisoned in the Tower of London.

Lady Jane Grey is often referred to as 'the Nine Day Queen' as it was nine days between the proclamation of her accession and her removal from power. She was never crowned queen. On 19th July 1553, the Privy Council of England named Mary as Queen of England, deposing Jane. Lady Jane Grey languished in the Tower of London, and was executed in February 1554.

QUEEN MARY I

REIGNED: 1553-1558

MARY was thirty-seven when she was crowned Queen Mary I. She was not married when she became monarch. Like her mother, Catherine of Aragon, Queen Mary I was a devout Catholic. Much of the population was delighted when Mary was crowned queen. They didn't like all the religious changes that had taken place during King Edward VI's reign. However, others wanted the Church to remain Protestant.

Soon after becoming queen, Mary married Philip II of Spain, who was also Catholic. Such a marriage jeopardised the English Reformation and made England one of the strongest Catholic states in Europe.

Mary started to undo all the religious changes her father and brother had implemented. She made England a Catholic country once more. Married priests were made to leave their wives, churches were redecorated, and church services and prayer books were once again written and read in Latin, not English.

Mary's changes didn't please Protestant worshippers. Mary had a brutal solution for the Protestant demonstrators. If Protestant congregants did not revert to Catholicism, Mary burnt them alive for heresy. More than two hundred people died in this way for their beliefs, including five bishops and twenty-one ministers. Mary earned herself the nickname 'Bloody Mary' because of this.

Mary I died in 1558. Her marriage to Philip II produced no children.

This colouring page is based on the famous Antonis Mor portrait from 1554.

QUEEN ELIZABETH I

REIGNED: 1558-1603

MARY'S YOUNGER HALF-SISTER, ELIZABETH, became Queen Elizabeth I in 1558. She was crowned at Westminster Abbey on the 15th January 1559. Elizabeth had many problems to solve.

England was in religious turmoil after the reigns of her half-siblings Edward VI and Mary I. Elizabeth planned to return the country to the Protestant faith, but had no intention of repeating the chaos caused by her half-brother and half-sister. Elizabeth wanted to avoid the extremes of both Catholics and Protestants. She wanted to keep the country a peaceful place and please most people. Her ideas were known as the Religious Settlement. Elizabeth made herself Governor, not Head of the Church of England. This meant that Catholics could still think of the pope as the head of the Church instead of her, if they wanted to.

Elizabeth knew that she had to get people on her side. Some citizens said that Elizabeth was illegitimate, as the 1536 Act of Succession had ruled her so. Elizabeth toured the country and spoke to as many of her subjects as possible. For those who could not see her, the queen made sure they could see her picture, in Bibles, for example.

While Elizabeth was Queen of England, Scotland was a separate country with its own ruler, Elizabeth's first cousin once removed, Mary, Queen of Scots. Mary was the great-granddaughter of Henry VII and a strong claimant to the English throne. She was overtly Catholic. In 1565, Mary married Lord Darnley, and they had a son, James. A year later, Darnley was murdered, and Mary married his assumed murderer, Lord Bothwell. Within three months, Mary's court demanded she abdicate in favour of her one-year-old son James. Mary escaped from imprisonment and fled south to England, hoping that her cousin Elizabeth I would give her sanctuary and protect her. To her shock, Mary was apprehended and imprisoned shortly after she crossed the border.

During her imprisonment, Mary received numerous letters from Catholics in England and Spain, full of plans to set her free, murder Elizabeth, and crown Mary as the new Catholic Queen of England. Mary was implicated in three of these plans, and the fourth, in 1586, cost her her life. Mary, Queen of Scots, was tried, convicted and executed for treason in 1587.

Elizabeth won a decisive victory over the Spanish Armada in 1588. Elizabeth's long reign of forty-four years firmly established the Protestant faith as the dominant religion in England above Catholicism.

Elizabeth I died in 1603 with no children. She never married and is often referred to as the Virgin Queen. Elizabeth I was the last monarch of the Tudor Dynasty. Her reign was known as the Golden Age.

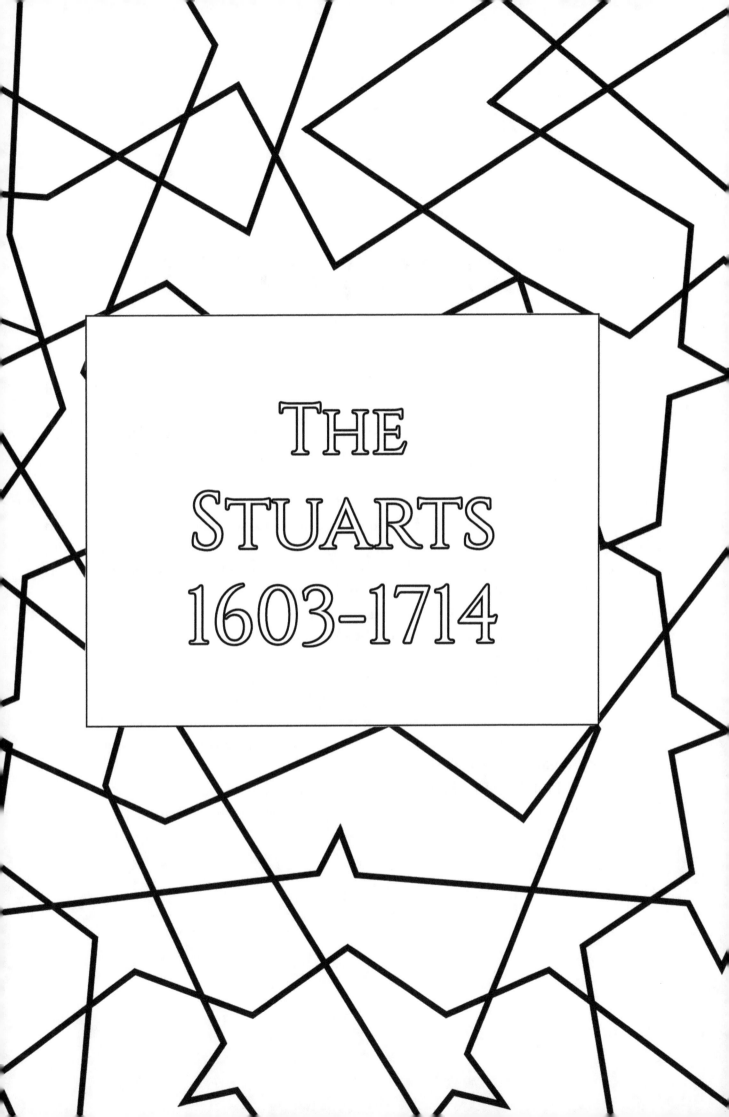

THE STUARTS 1603-1714

KING JAMES I

REIGNED: 1603-1625

IN 1603, KING JAMES VI OF SCOTLAND, son of Mary, Queen of Scots, became King James I of England. James inherited the English throne following Elizabeth I's death. Like Elizabeth, Mary, Queen of Scots was descended from King Henry VII, but via his eldest daughter, Margaret Tudor, and James was the great-great-grandson of King Henry VII.

James I was the first English monarch of the Stuart dynasty.

When James became King of England, Scotland remained independent. Scotland had its own Parliament and privy council. James did not allow the Scots full trading rights with England. Scottish merchants paid taxes on goods they brought into England. The Scots were also denied trading rights with the growing British Empire.

To the English, James was an outsider from an enemy state. James believed in a king's divine right to rule, having been chosen by God. In 1605, a group of radicals reacted to James I's reign by taking the drastic step of plotting to blow up Parliament. When one of the conspirators warned a friend to stay away from Parliament on its opening, Westminster was searched thoroughly, and on the night of 5th November 1605, a man named Guy Fawkes was caught with forty barrels of gunpowder in a cellar. If the gunpowder had been ignited and exploded while the king was in Parliament, there is little question that King James I would have been killed.

James I ruled England for twenty-two years. He died in 1625.

This colouring page is based on the famous Daniel Mytens portrait of James I from around 1621.

KING CHARLES I

REIGNED: 1625-1649

CHARLES I ascended to the throne upon the death of his father, James I. Like his father, King Charles I believed that kings were chosen to rule by God.

Charles quarrelled with Parliament shortly after becoming king. He needed money to run the country, and Parliament refused to grant him money. Charles managed to get money in other ways. He ordered wealthy people to lend him money and, if they refused, he put them in prison until they obeyed. War broke out, and Charles called another Parliament in 1628. Before it would give him money, Charles was forced to sign a document called the Petition of Rights. This forbade Charles from putting anyone unlawfully in prison, and he could not collect taxes without Parliament's permission. Charles continued to do both these things after signing the petition and even imprisoned some Members of Parliament.

Charles's battle for power and control with Parliament lasted for the next fourteen years, with parliaments dismissed, dissolved and formed in this period. In January 1642, Charles made one last attempt to control Parliament. The king arrived in the House of Commons with a group of soldiers. He was determined to arrest his five main opponents. The attempted arrest was unsuccessful. The five Parliamentary members had heard of the arrest plan and managed to escape. Shortly afterwards, Charles left London and travelled north. He appealed to all of his subjects of age to join him and fight Parliament. Meanwhile, in London, Parliament began to raise an army. Civil war had begun in England.

Parliament had several advantages in the Civil War. Firstly, it controlled the wealthiest part of England, London. Secondly, the navy had sided with Parliament. This prevented Charles from getting soldiers and supplies from abroad. Finally, Parliament produced much better military commanders than Charles. The most successful of these commanders was Oliver Cromwell. Cromwell promoted people for their talent and ability rather than their religious belief or their wealth. When Scotland joined Parliament's side in 1643, the king's cause was greatly weakened. In 1646, King Charles I surrendered to the Scottish army, who sold the monarch to Parliament in London.

In 1649, Charles was charged with murder, treason and tyranny. Charles believed in the divine right of kings and monarchy and would not accept the trial was legal. He refused to defend himself. King Charles I was declared guilty and beheaded three days later.

This colouring page is based on the famous Daniel Mytens portrait of Charles I from 1629.

KING CHARLES II

REIGNED: 1660-1685

AFTER CHARLES I'S EXECUTION on 30th January 1649, the country was ruled by Parliament and Oliver Cromwell. Cromwell's strict religious views didn't make him popular. He banned most sports and closed down pubs and theatres. He even cancelled Christmas and Easter and replaced them with days of fasting.

Oliver Cromwell died in 1658. In April 1660, Parliament asked Charles II, son of King Charles I, to return from exile and become king. This was called the Restoration of the Monarchy.

Charles II was known as the 'Merry Monarch'. He brought back sports and entertainment and could often be seen racing down the River Thames in his yacht.

Charles decided to kill the men who had killed his father. Fifty-nine people had signed King Charles I's death warrant in 1649, and Charles II was convinced they had all committed regicide. Oliver Cromwell was already dead. Charles demanded that Cromwell's body be taken out of its coffin and publicly hanged at Tyburn. Cromwell's decomposing head was then cut off his corpse and publicly placed on a pole for over twenty years.

Charles II's reign was not an easy one. He was monarch during the Great Fire of London in 1666 and during the bubonic plague in 1665, which killed almost 70,000 people in London in just eight months.

Charles was careful to build a good relationship with Parliament as he didn't want another civil war. Although this was the case, like his father, Charles did not like ruling with a parliament. England was now firmly a protestant country. In 1670, Charles II secretly promised the King of France, Louis XIV, that he would make England a Roman Catholic country again.

This colouring page is based on the famous Philippe De Champaigne portrait of Charles II from 1653.

KING JAMES II

REIGNED: 1685-1688

CHARLES II had a fit in February 1685, and died shortly afterwards. The crown passed to his younger brother, James, who was crowned King James II.

James II was openly Roman Catholic. In 1685, most people in Britain were Protestant. James allowed Catholics to worship freely. People were alarmed by this, but at fifty-one, James was getting old, and it was expected that he would die soon. People thought that he would be succeeded by his Protestant daughter, Mary.

James used his power as king to give top jobs in the army and government to Catholics. He proclaimed in a speech in 1687 that he wished all his subjects were Catholic. Like his father, King Charles I, James dissolved Parliament in 1687. But, as was the case in his father's reign, the populace was getting tired of James.

Then, in 1688, the unthinkable happened; James's Catholic wife gave birth to a baby boy. As the child was male, he superseded James's Protestant daughter, Mary, in the line of succession. Protestants were horrified. The new prince would be brought up as Catholic, and so would his sons, and so on. Parliament didn't want this, so they decided to do something about it.

Parliament's plan was for James's Protestant daughter, Mary, and her Protestant husband, William of Orange, to gather an army and fight King James II. Once victorious, they would then become joint king and queen. Mary agreed to fight her father. Mary and William landed in Devon on 5th November 1688. Only a few English people supported James, and they were called Jacobites. James realised that he couldn't beat his daughter and fled to France. There wasn't any fighting, but a revolution had taken place. Today, this is known as the Glorious Revolution.

James II was the last Catholic monarch to rule England.

This colouring page is based on the portrait of James II from 1690 by an unknown artist .

KING WILLIAM III & QUEEN MARY II

REIGNED: 1689-1702

W ILLIAM III had not inherited the throne; Parliament had handed him the crown. Consequently, in 1689, William III and Mary II agreed to the Bill of Rights drafted by Parliament. The monarchs promised to obey the law and call frequent parliaments. Furthermore, the Bill of Rights allowed Parliament to control their money. This kind of rule with limits is called a constitutional monarchy.

The Bill of Rights was a major turning point in British Regal history. The struggle exacerbated in the days of King Charles I between Parliament and the monarch was over. The Bill of Rights made Parliament more powerful than any king or queen. Monarchs could now be appointed by Parliament and had to abide by the rules that Parliament created.

Queen Mary II died of smallpox at Kensington Palace in December 1694, leaving William to rule alone. William continued to rule England until his death in March 1702.

William and Mary were childless, so Parliament passed a law that named Mary's younger Protestant sister, Anne, as the next queen when William died.

This colouring page is based on the Thomas Murray portrait of William III from 1691.

QUEEN ANNE

REIGNED: 1702-1714

IN 1702 WHEN WILLIAM III DIED, Anne became Queen of England.

Anne gave birth to seventeen children during her lifetime, but tragically, they all died. Anne's seventeen pregnancies by her husband George resulted in twelve miscarriages or stillbirths, four infant deaths and a persistently sick son, William, who died at the age of eleven. Parliament was concerned that the crown would pass onto her younger Catholic brother if Anne died without a Protestant heir. With James II's Catholic rule still fresh in their minds, Parliament passed a law called the Act of the Settlement. This law stated that the crown would be passed onto Anne's nearest Protestant relative after her death if she died with no surviving issue. The Bill of Rights allowed Parliament to pass this law.

To make the country even more secure, Parliament passed the Act of Union in 1707. This meant that England, Wales, Scotland and Ireland were all united with one Parliament based in London. Queen Anne, therefore, was the first monarch to call herself Queen of Great Britain and Ireland.

Queen Anne's husband, Prince George of Denmark, died in 1708.

Anne ruled for twelve years. She died in 1714 and was said to be an extremely large lady at her death. Queen Anne was the last Stuart monarch and died with no living heir.

This colouring page is based on the famous John Closterman portrait of Queen Anne from around 1702.

THE HOUSE OF HANOVER
1714–1901

KING GEORGE I

REIGNED: 1714-1727

FOLLOWING THE ACT OF SETTLEMENT, Queen Anne's nearest Protestant relative at the time of her death was her second cousin, George of Hanover. However, George was from Germany and could not speak any English. Although this was the case, following the Act of Settlement, George became Britain's king on 1ˢᵗ August 1714 and was crowned King George I.

As happened in 1603, when King James VI of Scotland became King of England, many people were not happy when George, a foreigner who could not speak the common tongue, took the throne. The majority of the population wanted Queen Anne's half-brother, James Stuart, to be king instead. The people who supported James were called Jacobites.

The Act of Settlement prevented James from becoming king because he was Catholic. However, James had strong support, particularly in Scotland. In 1715, James decided to rebel against King George I. He landed in Peterhead in Scotland and gathered a large army. Despite his large army, James was defeated by George. James fled to Rome and never returned to Britain again.

George I was the first monarch of the House of Hanover. He ruled Britain until he died in 1727. The king died of a stroke on a trip to Hanover. George I was buried in Hanover and is the most recent British monarch to be buried outside the United Kingdom.

This colouring page is based on the famous Sir Godfrey Kneller portrait of George I from around 1714.

KING GEORGE II

REIGNED: 1727-1760

KING GEORGE I'S SON, also called George, ascended to the throne as King George II upon his father's death.

The years between 1715-1745 were years of prosperity and peace in Britain. Unfortunately, this was not to last. In 1745, George II was confronted by the second Jacobite Rebellion.

James Stuart's son, Charles Edward Stuart, who was the grandson of King James II and a living heir of the House of Stuart, had a legitimate claim to the British throne. Charles, who had been brought up in Rome and had never been in Britain, landed in Scotland in July 1745, determined to take the British throne from George II.

Charles quickly won control of Scotland. His army marched south to Carlisle, then to Manchester, then to Derby. Charles was 130 miles north of London, but he failed to get the support he needed in Derby. Consequently, he and his men were forced to march back to Scotland.

In April 1746, George's army caught up with Charles and the Jacobites at Culloden. A battle ensued. The Jacobites were outnumbered two to one by the king's army. The Jacobites were slaughtered, although Charles managed to escape from the battlefield. He fled to France dressed as a woman. Charles would never again return to Britain. He became an alcoholic and died in 1788.

King George II had crushed the rebellion and cemented the reign of the House of Hanover. He ruled as monarch for thirty-three years and died aged seventy-seven in 1760. At the time of his death, King George II had lived longer than any of his English or British predecessors.

This colouring page is based on the famous Charles Jervas portrait of George II from around 1727.

KING GEORGE III

REIGNED: 1760-1820

GEORGE II was not replaced by his son, Frederick, as he had predeceased him, but by his grandson, the twenty-two-year-old George III.

King George III boasted that he was a true-born Englishman, not a German immigrant. He was monarch during the Industrial Revolution, a time when the population of England, Scotland and Wales had almost doubled - from five million at the start of the century to nearly ten million.

On 4th July 1776, Thomas Jefferson published a Declaration of Independence, declaring George III 'unfit to be the ruler of free people'. Thirteen American colonies were no longer subject and subordinate to the British monarch, and the United States of America was born. Britain had lost America, not to a rival European power but to something more humiliating and more radical, self-government.

In 1809, George III subsided into mental illness. The king would be plagued by mental health issues for the remainder of his life. Due to the country lacking a coherent leader, George III's son, George, Prince of Wales, was declared Prince Regent in 1811.

George III died in 1820. At the time of his death, he was blind, deaf and insane. He is sometimes referred to as the mad king.

This colouring page is based on the Johann Zoffany portrait of George III from 1771.

KING GEORGE IV

REIGNED: 1820-1830

GEORGE IV was crowned in 1820. He had been ruling the country for the previous nine years as Prince Regent.

King George IV was obsessed with glamour and splendour. His coronation saw him cloaked in a costume copied from the French emperor's robes.

George remodelled Buckingham House into Buckingham Palace, where the Royal Family resides today.

During George's reign, the population in Britain continued to grow. Improved nutrition meant that people lived longer. New industrial cities such as Leeds, Birmingham and Manchester appeared alongside old cathedral cities. Britain had become the world's first industrial nation. Crime rose. To combat this, an unarmed Metropolitan Police Force was founded in London.

The country was changing radically. George IV detested the new liberalism.

George IV died in 1830 at Windsor. He was an unpopular monarch at the time of his death.

This colouring page is based on the famous Sir Thomas Lawrence coronation portrait of George IV.

KING WILLIAM IV

REIGNED: 1830-1837

GEORGE IV had no surviving children at the time of his death. George IV's daughter, Princess Charlotte, had died in 1817, predeceasing both her father and her grandfather, George III. Her death was met with great sadness. Charlotte was seen as a sign of hope for the monarchy and a contrast to her unpopular father and mad grandfather.

When George died, the British throne was passed onto George's sixty-four-year-old brother, William.

William IV was a successful naval officer, having served as Lord Admiral, and was not keen on becoming king. He had ten children by his long-standing mistress, an actress named Dorothea Jordan. None of his children were viewed as legitimate in the line of succession.

William IV died at Windsor Castle in 1837, having ruled for seven years. He died with no legitimate issue. William IV was the last king of the House of Hanover.

This colouring page is based on the famous Sir Martin Archer Shee portrait of William IV.

QUEEN VICTORIA

REIGNED: 1837-1901

IN 1837, QUEEN VICTORIA inherited the crown upon the death of her uncle, King William IV. Victoria was the only child of King George III's fourth son, Prince Edward, Duke of Kent.

Victoria was told of the death of her uncle by the Archbishop of Canterbury and the lord chamberlain, who woke her up at 5.a.m. at Kensington Palace. She was barely out of her nightdress when she was told the news.

The Industrial Revolution continued during Victoria's reign and by now had moved far beyond the eighteenth-century centres of textile manufacture. In the 1840s, thousands of miles of railway track were laid across the country.

In 1848, Europe's year of revolutions saw monarchies toppled in France, Italy, Poland and Austria. However, the British monarchy and Queen Victoria survived.

In 1861, Victoria's husband, Prince Albert, died. The queen was grief-stricken. She plunged into what seemed eternal mourning, dressing in black and keeping his portrait on his pillow next to hers when she slept. Victoria rarely made public appearances after her beloved Albert's death.

In 1858, the British Raj was enacted. This enacted the rule by the British Crown on the Indian subcontinent. In 1876, Victoria was declared Empress of India.

On 22nd January 1901, Queen Victoria died. She had nine children, many of whom married into European Royal Families. To most Britons, Victoria offered what they had long craved for in a monarch, stability and continuity. Queen Victoria's reign is referred to as the Victorian era. She was the last monarch of the House of Hanover.

This colouring page is based on the famous Franz Xaver Winterhalter portrait of Queen Victoria.

The House of Windsor
Saxe-Coburg Gotha
1901-Present

KING EDWARD VII

REIGNED: 1901-1910

EDWARD VII was crowned King of Britain and Emperor of India in 1901 after the death of his mother, Queen Victoria.

During his reign, technical innovation in France and Germany were overtaking that of Britain. King Edward VII's first two cars were a French Renault and a German Mercedes. And three emergent twentieth-century industries – cinema, cars, and aviation– were being led from across the Atlantic.

Edward VII died in 1910. His funeral was described as the greatest assembly of royalty and rank ever gathered in one place. Many of his extended family came from across Europe, and those present would soon be at war with each other during World War I.

Edward's reign is known as the Edwardian era.

This colouring page is based on the famous Sir (Samuel) Luke Fildes portrait of Edward VII from around 1902.

KING GEORGE V

REIGNED: 1910-1936

IN 1910, GEORGE V was crowned King of Britain and Emperor of India after the death of his father, King Edward VII. He was Edward's second son. His older brother, Prince Albert Victor, predeceased their father and died in 1892. George V was born during the reign of his grandmother, Queen Victoria.

In 1911, the Parliament Act established the supremacy of the elected British House of Commons over the unelected House of Lords.

George V was King of Britain during World War I. In 1917, George became the first monarch of the House of Windsor. He changed the name of the Royal house from the House of Saxe-Coburg and Gotha to Windsor due to anti-German public sentiment during World War I.

George V was a heavy smoker. In the early twentieth century, smoking was popular and almost fashionable. In George's era, people were oblivious to the detrimental health problems caused by smoking. George suffered from chronic bronchitis and breathing problems throughout his life. In his final year, he was occasionally administered oxygen. George V died in 1936.

This colouring page is based on the famous Sir (Samuel) Luke Fildes portrait of George V from 1911.

KING EDWARD VIII

REIGNED: 20TH JANUARY - 11TH DECEMBER 1936

GEORGE V was succeeded by his forty-one-year-old son, King Edward VIII.
Edward liked dancing and informality. He took a keen interest in public life.

Just months into Edward VIII's reign, a constitutional crisis was caused by his decision to marry Wallis Simpson. Simpson was an American woman who had divorced her first husband and sought a divorce from her second husband. The king was given an ultimatum: he would have to choose between Simpson and the Crown.

The monarchy no longer carried the political weight or power it did before William III and Mary II signed the Bill of Rights in 1689. Although Edward VIII enjoyed some public support, the exemplary role a king must play in public life made his relationship with Simpson unacceptable.

In a television broadcast on 11th December 1936, Edward VIII chose Wallis Simpson over the crown, and abdicated. Edward was created Duke of Windsor, and married Simpson in France six months later, after her second divorce was finalised.

This colouring page is based on the famous Albert H Collings portrait of Edward VIII.

KING GEORGE VI

REIGNED: 1936-1952

EDWARD VIII was succeeded by his younger brother, Albert, who was crowned King George VI. George was the father of the present queen, Elizabeth II. He was born during the reign of his great-grandmother, Queen Victoria.

George VI was King of Britain during World War II. Along with Prime Minister Winston Churchill, King George and his wife, Elizabeth, became symbols of resistance during World War II when, rather than flee London, they were filmed viewing bomb damage at Buckingham Palace.

When World War II concluded in 1945, George VI was viewed as a national hero.

George VI was the last Emperor of India. In 1947, the British Raj was dissolved. Britain's hold on the globe was beginning to diminish, and the British Empire was declining.

Like his father, George V, George VI was a heavy smoker. In 1952, aged fifty-six, King George VI died in his sleep at Sandringham House in Norfolk.

QUEEN ELIZABETH II

REIGNED: 1952 - PRESENT

On 31ST JANUARY 1952, Princess Elizabeth set off on her tour to Australia via Kenya. Six days later, King George VI died. Princess Elizabeth flew back to Britain from Kenya as Queen Elizabeth II.

Elizabeth II's coronation was the first national event shown on television. The pageantry and excitement were compared to the crowning of Queen Victoria in 1837.

To this day, Queen Elizabeth II is Queen of the United Kingdom and the following Commonwealth realms: Canada, Australia, New Zealand, Jamaica, Barbados, the Bahamas, Grenada, Solomon Islands, Papua New Guinea, Tuvalu, St Lucia, St Vincent and the Grenadines, Belize, Antigua and Barbuda, and St Kitts and Nevis.

In 2017, Elizabeth II became the first British monarch to celebrate a Sapphire Jubilee. She is the longest-reigning British monarch in history. Elizabeth II has four children: Prince Charles, Princess Anne, Prince Andrew and Prince Edward. In 2021, after seventy-three years of marriage, her husband, Prince Philip, died aged ninety-nine.

Queen Elizabeth II is a much-loved figure. Like Queen Victoria, Elizabeth II has brought a long period of stability and continuity to Britain and the monarchy.

THE FUTURE OF THE BRITISH MONARCHY

THE HOUSE OF WINDSOR appears to have secured the future of the British monarchy. Charles, Prince of Wales, is next in the line of succession to the British throne. Charles is the oldest and longest-serving heir apparent in British history. His son, Prince William, Duke of Cambridge, is second in the line of succession to the British throne; and William's son, Prince George of Cambridge, is third in the line of succession to the British throne.

SOURCES

Adams, R. et al (2003) 'Think History! Revolutionary Times 1500-1750'.

Carter, M. et al (1990) 'Past into Present 2 1400-1700'.

Clare, J (1997) 'A United Kingdom' 1500-1750'

Jenkins, S (2011, 2012) 'A Short History of England'

Murphy, D et al (2010) 'Collins History Book 2: 1750-1918'.

Pearl, R (2016) 'Medieval Britain 410-1509'

Wilkes, A (2014) 'Renaissance, Revolution and Reformation Britain 1509-1745'.

Whitehall, D (1990) 'The Past in Question Life in Elizabethan Times'.

MEET THE
AUTHOR AND ILLUSTRATOR

Joseph Stephen is an illustrator and author with an avid interest in British history, particularly the Tudor period. Joseph lives in the United Kingdom and studied Criminology and Law at Coventry University. He started his own children's e-commerce business, PJ Scribbles, during the Covid-19 pandemic, and this led him to publish a colouring book to combine his skills as an artist with his passion for Tudor history.

Joseph has always had a passion for drawing and the arts and recently began working with MadeGlobal Publishing. He is the author and illustrator of the *Kings and Queens of England and Great Britain Colouring Book* and *How to Draw The Tudor Kings and Queens*.

Debra Bayani, author of Jasper Tudor: Godfather of the Tudor Dynasty, and artist **Dmitry Yakhovsky** have come together to create this beautiful colouring book which will be enjoyed by both young and old.

The Wars of the Roses lasted for over thirty years and were a series of civil wars fought between rival claimants for the English throne: the Yorkists and Lancastrians. This tumultuous period of history saw the rise of some fascinating historical personalities, and the downfall of others, bloody battles, rebellions, murders, betrayal, and finally the unification of the warring factions.

In **The Wars of the Roses Colouring Book**, Debra's text introduces these main characters, events and places, while Dmitry's stunning artwork and your colouring will bring them to life. Relax, unwind and express yourself, all while learning about the Wars of the Roses

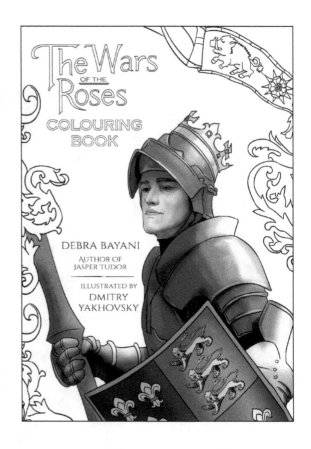

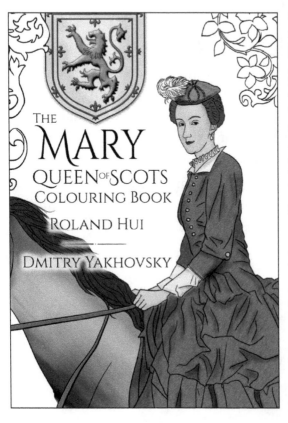

Queen of Scotland by birth, Queen of France by marriage, and Queen of England by right (some said), the life of Mary Stuart (1542-1587) was the stuff of legend. A monarch at only six days old, Mary's early years were spent at the glittering court of France. Pampered and Indulged, she was little prepared for what lay ahead upon her return to Scotland to take up the reins of power. Murder, scandal, and betrayal would send her fleeing to England to seek the help of her cousin, Queen Elizabeth. Mary's fateful journey, which began with so much hope, would lead to her greatest tragedy.

Roland Hui, author of The Turbulent Crown - The Story of the Tudor Queens, and artist **Dmitry Yakhovsky** have come together to create a beautiful colouring book which will be enjoyed by all ages. In **The Mary, Queen of Scots Colouring Book**, Roland Hui's text introduces the characters, events, and places of this absorbing drama, while Dmitry Yakhovsky's stunning artwork and your colouring bring them to life. Relax, unwind, and express yourself while learning about the exciting and moving life of the fascinating Mary Stuart.

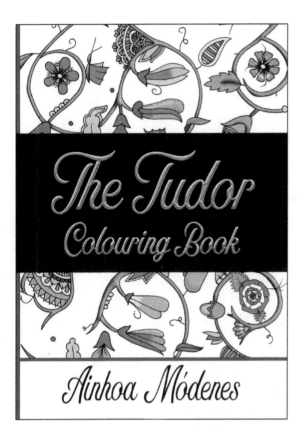

Talented artist **Ainhoa Módenes** brings together popular mandalas and patterns from the Tudor period to create unique and beautiful colouring designs.

Colouring is known to both inspire and relax the mind, so grab your choice of pencils or pens and enjoy completing these 42 Tudor-inspired, hand-drawn illustrations.

Each colouring is on a separate page and is accompanied by text explaining the inspiration behind it, whether it's Tudor architecture, embroidery, heraldry, illuminations or portraits.

The Tudor Colouring Book will provide hours of joy, inspiration and relaxation. Foreword and accompanying text by Claire Ridgway, author of eight history books.

Claire Ridgway, author of The Fall of Anne Boleyn: A Countdown and owner of The Anne Boleyn Files website, and artist **Dmitry Yakhovsky** have come together to create this beautiful colouring book which will be enjoyed by young and old alike.

The Life of Anne Boleyn Colouring Book tells Anne Boleyn's story through both text and drawings, from her family background, through her rise and fall at Henry VIII's court, to her execution in May 1536, and her legacy: Queen Elizabeth I. Learn all about Anne Boleyn while Dmitry's stunning illustrations and your colouring bring Anne, her story and other famous Tudor characters to life. This book is a fitting tribute to Queen Anne Boleyn.

Relax, unwind and express yourself with these 34 colouring pages. Each colouring is accompanied by a page of text giving an accurate account of Anne Boleyn's life.

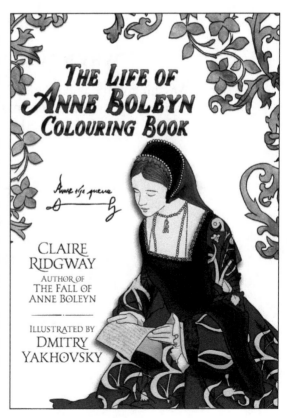

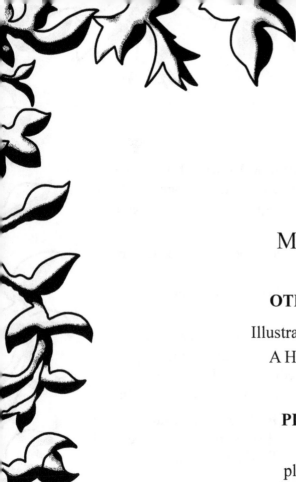

MadeGlobal Publishing

OTHER MONARCHY BOOKS:

Illustrated Kings and Queens of England
A History of the English Monarchy
The Turbulent Crown

PLEASE LEAVE A REVIEW

If you enjoyed this book,
please leave a review on Amazon
or at the book seller where you purchased it.
There is no better way to thank the author
and it really does make a huge difference!
Thank you in advance.

VISIT OUR SITE

https://www.madeglobalpublishing.com
for more books from other authors

WHY NOT SHARE YOUR COLOURING?

Anything in life is possible if you put your mind to it. Use your talents and
your gifts, embrace your passions, let your magic and creativity flow,
and the world will give back to you tenfold.

Please share the pages as you do them via any of these
social media channels:
https://www.facebook.com/madeglobalpublishing
https://twitter.com/madeglobal
Instagram: MadeGlobal

Happy colouring!

Printed in the USA
CPSIA information can be obtained
at www.ICGtesting.com
LVHW062349250823
756290LV00009B/651